9/9/04

ALLOSAURUS

By Susan H. Gray

THE CHILD'S WORLD®
CHANHASSEN

The Child's World

Published in the United States of America by The Child's World®
PO Box 326, Chanhassen, MN 55317-0326
800-599-READ
www.childsworld.com

*Content Adviser:
Peter Makovicky,
Ph.D., Curator,
Field Museum,
Chicago, Illinois*

Photo Credits: American Museum of Natural History: 7; Corbis: 10-bottom (Michael S. Yamashita), 18 (AFP), 21 (Richard Cummins), 23 (Karl Ammann); Douglas Henderson: 27; Getty Images/Hulton Archive: 12; Michael Skrepnick: 24, 26; Mike Fredericks: 8; North Wind Picture Archive: 13; Photo Researchers: 11 (Jim Steinberg), 19 (Sinclair Stammers), 20 (Science Photo Library/Chris Butler); Photo Researchers/ François Gohier: 15, 17; Todd Marshall: 4-5, 22; Visuals Unlimited: 9 (Ken Lucas), 10-top (Albert Copley).

The Child's World®: Mary Berendes, Publishing Director

Editorial Directions, Inc.: E. Russell Primm, Editorial Director; Ruth M. Martin, Line Editor; Katie Marsico, Assistant Editor; Matthew Messbarger, Editorial Assistant; Susan Hindman, Copy Editor; Susan Ashley, Proofreader; Tim Griffin, Indexer; Kerry Reid, Fact Checker; Cian Loughlin O'Day, Photo Reseacher; Linda S. Koutris, Photo Selector

Original cover art by Todd Marshall

The Design Lab: Kathleen Petelinsek, Design and Art Direction; Kari Thornborough, Page Production

Library of Congress Cataloging-in-Publication Data
Gray, Susan Heinrichs.
  Allosaurus / by Susan H. Gray.
      p. cm. — (Exploring dinosaurs)
Includes index.
Contents: Too late for dinner—What is an Allosaurus?—Who found the first Allosaurus?—Who is Big Al?—How did Allosaurus spend its time?—Why isn't Allosaurus alive today?
  ISBN 1-59296-184-3 (lib. bdg. : alk. paper)
  1. Allosaurus—Juvenile literature. [1. Allosaurus. 2. Dinosaurs.] I. Title. II. Series.
QE862.S3G69 2004
567.912—dc22   2003018623

TABLE OF CONTENTS

CHAPTER ONE

Too Late for Dinner

Allosaurus (AL-oh-SAWR-russ) squinted his eyes and peered across the land. His mouth was as dry as dust. His chest was sunken, and his ribs pressed against his skin. His eyes were dull, and his heavy head drooped. *Allosaurus* had not had a decent meal in two weeks.

Suddenly, he spied a young dinosaur in the distance. It had wandered away from its herd and was lost. The youngster would be an easy meal for a big, flesh-eating **reptile** like himself.

Allosaurus lifted his head and began trotting toward the lone dinosaur. But running was agony. One of his toes was badly cut, so every step was painful. An infection made his shoulder ache as he limped. The ribs he had broken last year had not healed

A family of Allosaurus *attacking a young* Camarasaurus. *Scientists believe* Allosaurus *may have hunted in groups to overtake larger animals.*

properly. They made it hard for him to breathe as he ran. Still, this was his one chance to eat. He lumbered on.

All of a sudden, he heard something behind him. Another *Allosaurus* had also seen the lost dinosaur. This *Allosaurus* was young and healthy—and fast. He easily passed the wounded dinosaur and caught up with the lost youngster. One quick snap of the jaws and the dinner was his!

By the time the sick *Allosaurus* arrived, only a few bites remained. He helped himself, then stood upright. He was still starving. Again, he squinted his eyes and looked around. He needed a real meal. And he needed it soon.

CHAPTER TWO

WHAT IS AN ALLOSAURUS?

An *Allosaurus* is a dinosaur that lived from about 156 million to 144 million years ago. Its name is taken from Greek words that mean "different lizard" or "other lizard." The dinosaur was different because it had unusual bones in its spine. At the time the bones were discovered, their size and shape were very different from those of other known dinosaurs.

From the tip of its snout to the end of its tail, *Allosaurus* was up to 45 feet (14 meters) long. The animal had a thick, strong neck. Its head was huge

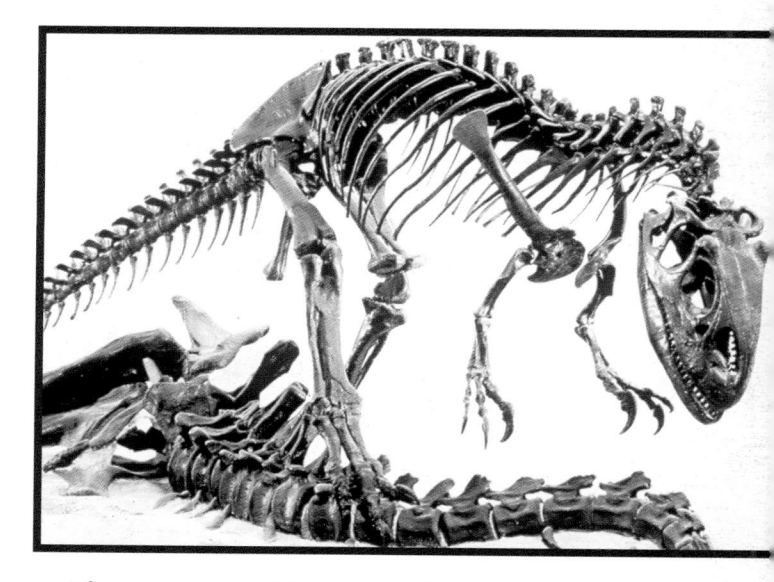

This reconstructed Allosaurus *skeleton is positioned over the partial skeleton of another dinosaur. Despite being different because of the shape and size of its spinal bones,* Allosaurus *was one of the most common meat-eating dinosaurs of its time.*

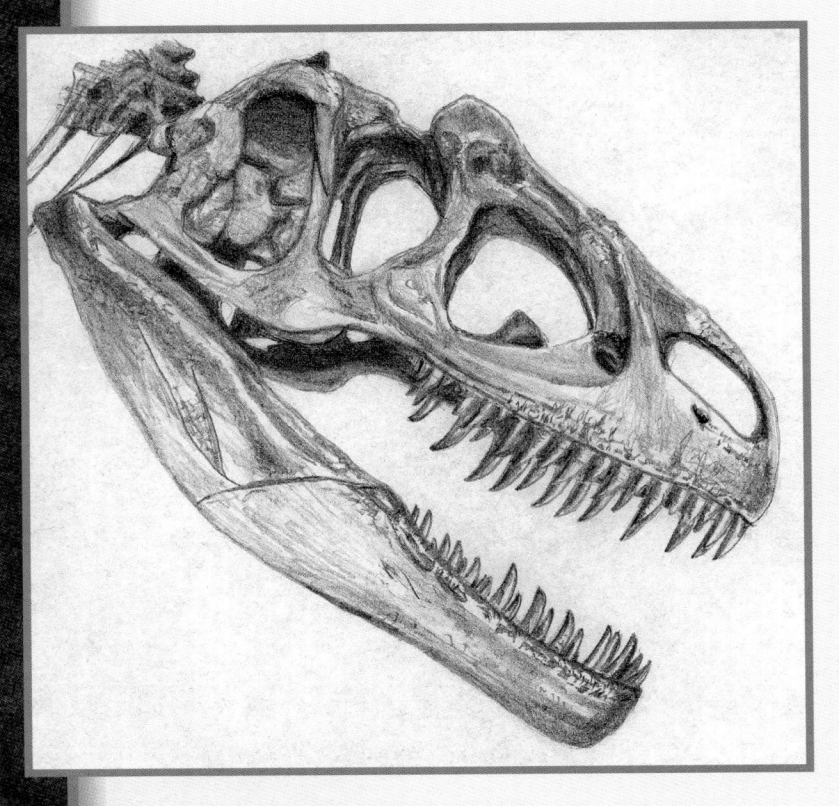

and could be up to 3 feet (1 m) in length. The head might have been too heavy to hold up if it weren't for the many holes and spaces in its skull.

Several bumps, knobs, and ridges rose from the dinosaur's

Scientists believe Allosaurus *used its strong neck muscles to drive its skull down into the flesh of an animal like a hatchet, or an axe. While the teeth of a* Tyrannosaurus rex *were more suited for crunching bones,* Allosaurus *probably used its teeth to tear chunks of flesh off of its unfortunate victim.*

face. Hard bumps sat just in front and in back of each eye. Low ridges ran from the eyes down to the snout.

Allosaurus's mouth was lined with teeth that grew up to 5 inches (13 centimeters) in length. The teeth were serrated (SEHR-rate-ed), or notched, like a saw blade. They curved backwards and were very sharp. The jaws were quite powerful and could open wide for big bites.

The reptile's arms were small for its body. Still, they were strong enough to hold on to its struggling **prey.** Each hand had

Some of the bumps and ridges near Allosaurus's eyes developed as the dinosaur grew older and may have been used to attract a mate.

Allosaurus's teeth were sharp—but not firmly rooted. While ripping at the flesh of its prey, Allosaurus *often lost its teeth, but was able to grow replacements.*

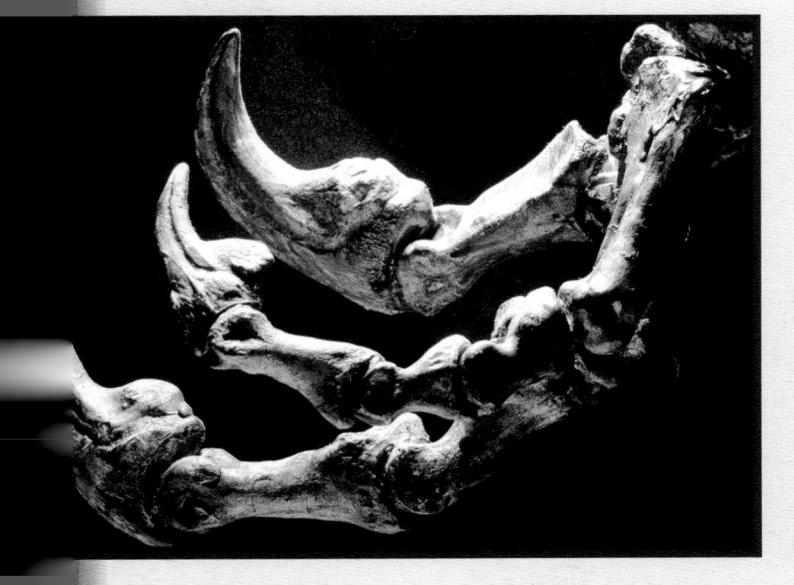

Allosaurus *had deadly claws on its hands that could grow up to 6 inches (15 cm) long! The claws on the dinosaur's feet were less curved and probably helped* Allosaurus *hold down its prey while it fed.*

three fingers, and each finger ended in a sharp, curved claw.

Allosaurus had mighty legs that could easily carry its gigantic body. An adult *Allosaurus* could weigh more than 3 tons. The dinosaur's powerful tail was almost as long as its body. As it walked about, *Allosaurus* probably lifted its tail off the ground to balance itself.

SPARE RIBS

Allosaurus had a big rib cage that protected its inner organs. The ribs were connected to the backbone and curved around the animal's sides. The dinosaur's heart and lungs sat inside its ribcage.

The reptile also had some extra riblike bones in the front of its chest and belly. These ribs were not connected to the backbone and they were not connected to other ribs. Instead, they were attached to the inside of the skin. Such ribs are called gastralia (gass-TRAY-lee-uh).

Gastralia may have helped protect the dinosaur's organs. Or they might have supported its belly. No one is quite sure of their purpose.

Allosaurus is not the only animal to have gastralia. Other dinosaurs and some ancient birds also had these ribs. Several modern lizards and crocodiles have them as well.

CHAPTER THREE

WHO FOUND THE FIRST ALLOSAURUS?

In the late 1860s, some people in Colorado found a bone they thought was an old horse hoof. It turned out to be a dinosaur bone, but it wasn't clear which dinosaur the bone belonged to.

In those days, paleontology (PAY-lee-un-TAWL-uh-jee) was very popular. Paleontology is the study of ancient living things. Paleontologists look for the **fossilized** remains of long-dead plants and animals. During the

Some scientists refer to late 1800s as the "golden age" of dinosaur paleontology because many of the prehistoric animals we know today were discovered and named in that period.

late 1800s, paleontologists in the western part of North America were finding all sorts of fossils. Newspapers reported their discoveries, and the public eagerly read the stories.

Paleontologists were the center of attention. One of them was Othniel Charles Marsh. He worked for a big museum in Connecticut, and his job was to find fossils.

Marsh sent out teams of fossil hunters to the western United States.

Othniel Charles Marsh was responsible for naming several dinosaurs, including Allosaurus, Apatosaurus, Diplodocus, Stegosaurus, *and* Triceratops.

He sent them out with cooks, food, camping supplies, picks, shovels, and even dynamite. Marsh told his men to do whatever it took to find dinosaur bones.

His teams were successful. They dug up many bones and sent them back to Marsh. A lot of the bones had crumbled and were in poor shape. But some bones clearly matched the old "horse hoof" bone. Marsh could see that these were from a new dinosaur. He gave it the name *Allosaurus*.

A few years later, in 1883, a man named M. P. Felch was working for Marsh. While fossil-hunting in Colorado, Felch made an incredible find. He discovered an almost complete skeleton of *Allosaurus*—and it was in great shape!

Since that time, thousands of *Allosaurus* fossils have been found in North America. Bones discovered in Australia, Portugal, and Africa might also be from *Allosaurus.* In some places, only fingers or toes have been found. In other places, nearly whole skeletons have been uncovered.

The Marsh/Felch Quarry is located in Canyon City, Colorado, and is where the first nearly complete Allosaurus *skeleton was discovered by M. P. Felch. Before Marsh hired him to search for dinosaur bones, Felch worked as a Colorado rancher. Felch didn't have much training as a paleontologist, but his hard work and careful observations led to an amazing discovery!*

CHAPTER FOUR

WHO IS BIG AL?

ig Al is the nickname of an *Allosaurus* found in Wyoming in 1991. Big Al was not all that huge. In fact, he was not quite fully grown when he died. However, he is "big" for another reason. Almost all of his bones were found, and his skull was in very good shape. An *Allosaurus* discovery that good was a *big* deal.

Paleontologists learned plenty about Big Al's life just by looking at his bones. His skeleton showed that he had lived a hard life. Big Al had suffered through broken ribs, broken tail bones, a broken leg, a serious toe infection, broken and infected fingers, shoulder problems, and a bad hip. And he wasn't even grown up yet!

An Allosaurus *skeleton on display at the College of Eastern Utah. Several* Allosaurus *fossils have been discovered in fairly decent condition. At one quarry in Utah, bones from at least 44 different* Allosaurus *(ranging in age from babies to full-grown adults) were unearthed.*

This tail bone once belonged to a relative of Allosaurus. Fossils tell us much about the past, but are often fragile and need to be handled carefully. Early paleontologists didn't always know this and sometimes broke or ruined valuable finds by treating them too roughly.

How did Big Al get all those injuries? People have come up with several ideas. Perhaps Big Al got knocked down by larger dinosaurs when he attacked them. Perhaps another *Allosaurus* fought with him over food. Or maybe Big Al was a little clumsy and often tripped and fell. Whatever caused his problems, it is clear that life was tough for this young dinosaur.

DINOSAUR DISEASES

How do we really know that dinosaurs were ever sick? How do we know they got infections? How do we know they healed from broken bones? When paleontologists wonder about the health of a dinosaur, they cannot go back in time to find out. They can only inspect the clues it left behind in its bones and teeth. They can also ask bone experts and tooth experts to take a look.

Sometimes, doctors and dentists are asked to study dinosaur remains. To do this, they might X-ray the teeth. They might look at the claws under a microscope. They might even take a bone to the hospital for a special scan.

Most diseases do not leave their marks on bones or teeth. But some do. For instance, bones that have been infected may not be as dense as healthy bones. They may also have odd lumps and holes. Bones that break and then heal also look different from normal bones. They grow

did not seem to get cavities, however. This is probably because the reptiles did not keep their teeth for very long. Old teeth were always falling out while new ones grew in.

Paleontologists have found dinosaur teeth with unusual worn spots. These tell scientists that the animal's teeth did not meet properly. The upper and lower teeth scraped each other as the dinosaur ate. Sometimes, scientists find a dinosaur bone with bite marks from another dinosaur. Such things must have been painful for both animals. One dinosaur got bitten, and the other dinosaur broke a tooth.

back thicker at the broken part. Sometimes they heal a little crooked.

Experts have found that dinosaurs often chipped or broke their teeth. This probably happened when they bit down on bones as they were eating. Dinosaurs

CHAPTER FIVE

HOW DID *ALLOSAURUS* SPEND ITS TIME?

Like most reptiles, *Allosaurus* probably spent much of its time sleeping, looking for water, finding a mate, and grooming itself. It also spent a lot of time hunting and eating.

Allosaurus was a large carnivore (KAR-nuh-vore). This means that it ate only the flesh of other animals. Everything about the dinosaur

This Allosaurus *fossil shows what the mighty prehistoric hunter looked like as it roamed about in search of food. Scientists believe* Allosaurus *fed on plant-eating dinosaurs, such as* Stegosaurus, Diplodocus, *and* Apatosaurus.

Allosaurus's jaws were hinged like those of a snake. This allowed the dinosaur to swallow huge chunks of its prey whole.

was suited for a meat-eating life. Its powerful back legs could help it

chase down slower prey. Its clawed hands could grip an animal while

its clawed feet tore at its flesh. Its large, loosely hinged jaws could open

wide to take big bites. And its backward-curving teeth could hold fast

to an animal trying to escape.

It might seem like *Allosaurus* must have caught every animal it

chased. But we know that is not the case. For one thing, *Allosaurus* may not have been a very speedy dinosaur. Some scientists believe it could run about 20 miles (32 kilometers) an hour. This is only a little faster than a modern elephant can run.

High-speed chases would have caused problems for *Allosaurus*. An animal that weighed 2 or 3 tons and raced around on only two legs might have had trouble with its balance. *Allosaurus* had an enormous head and a heavy tail.

Elephants can run at speeds of up to 15 miles (24 km) an hour. For many years, scientists didn't even acknowledge that elephants ran, and believed they could only move as fast as 10 miles (16 km) an hour.

Balancing those two weights as it ran could have been difficult. And if the dinosaur fell forward, its two little arms could not do much to stop the fall.

For these reasons, some paleontologists believe that *Allosaurus* went after small, slow, or sickly prey. Maybe it followed herds of other dinosaurs, waiting for one to drift away from the pack. Perhaps it even ate animals that had already died.

If it wasn't chasing a sickly, larger animal, Allosaurus *probably went after small prey such as* Dryosaurus. *This little plant-eater only weighed up to 200 pounds (90 kilograms) and measured 10 feet (3m) long.*

CHAPTER SIX

WHY ISN'T *ALLOSAURUS* ALIVE TODAY?

The last *Allosaurus* on Earth died about 144 million years ago. Since then, many kinds of dinosaurs have come and gone. After *Allosaurus* died out, other dinosaurs including *Iguanodon* (ig-WAH-nuh-don) appeared. *Iguanodon* was a large plant-eater. In time, *Iguanodon* died out and still other dinosaurs appeared, such as *Velociraptor* (vuh-LAHS-ih-RAP-ter). It was a speedy little **predator** that ran around on two legs.

Dinosaurs roamed the Earth for more than 160 million years. During that time, the world was constantly changing. Some areas warmed up. Other areas became cooler. Great landmasses shifted apart. Mountain ranges pushed up from flat lands. Volcanoes

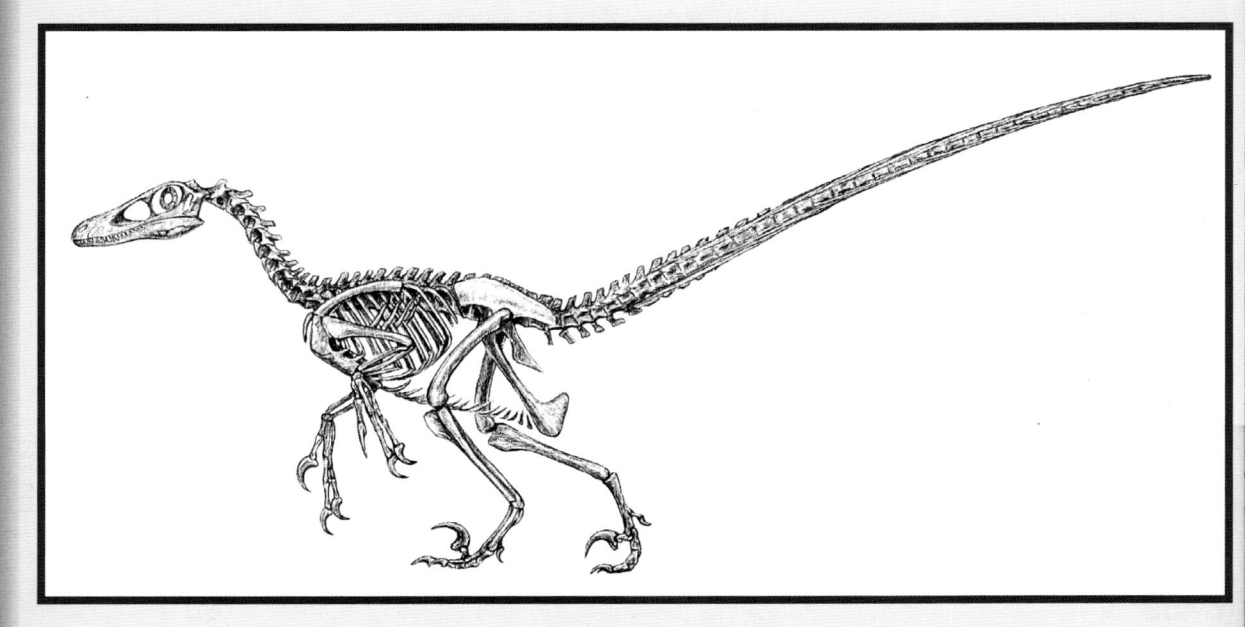

A drawing of a Velociraptor *skeleton.* Velociraptor *lived about 85 to 80 million years ago. It was known for its deadly claws, extra sharp teeth, and quick speed.*

erupted and became quiet again. Grasses and flowers appeared and spread everywhere.

As Earth changed, the types of dinosaurs changed. No one is sure exactly which changes forced *Allosaurus* and the other dinosaurs to become **extinct.** Perhaps some dinosaurs died out because they could not survive the temperature changes. Perhaps there were floods, **droughts**, or volcanic explosions. Maybe a shrinking food supply killed them.

The dinosaurs left no clear answers to these mysteries, but fossils give us valuable clues. We still have plenty to learn, so it is certain we will be studying these ancient creatures for years to come.

Some scientists believe that volcanoes killed off the dinosaurs. If clouds of volcanic ash blocked sunlight for long periods of time, plants wouldn't have been able to grow, and plant-eating dinosaurs would have died of hunger, followed by meat-eating predators.

Glossary

ancient (AYN-shunt) Something that is ancient is very old; from millions of years ago. Paleontology is the study of ancient plant and animal life.

droughts (DROWTS) Droughts are long periods of dry weather. A number of droughts might have caused some of the dinosaurs to become extinct.

extinct (ek-STINGKT) Something that is extinct no longer exists. The dinosaurs became extinct.

fossilized (FOSS-uhl-eyezed) Something that is fossilized became a fossil. Scientists might find fossilized plant matter where a dinosaur's stomach would have been.

predator (PRED-uh-tor) A predator is an animal that hunts and eats other animals. *Allosaurus* was a powerful predator.

prey (PRAY) Prey are animals that are hunted and eaten by other animals. Even though the *Allosaurus* had small arms, they would have been strong enough to hold on to its prey.

reptile (REP-tile) A reptile is an air-breathing animal with a backbone and is usually covered with scales or plates. *Allosaurus* was a reptile.

Did You Know?

▶ *Allosaurus* is the state fossil of Utah.

▶ When Big Al was dug up, schoolchildren in the area were let out of classes to go and watch. More than 4,000 students got to see the dinosaur being removed from the ground.

▶ Some people confuse *Allosaurus* with *Tyrannosaurus rex*. Both were meat eaters with big jaws and little arms. However, *Allosaurus* never saw a *T. rex* in its life. *T. rex* walked on Earth tens of millions of years after *Allosaurus* became extinct.

The Geologic Time Scale

TRIASSIC PERIOD

Date: 248 million to 208 million years ago

Fossils: *Coelophysis, Cynodont, Desmatosuchus, Eoraptor, Gerrothorax, Peteinosaurus, Placerias, Plateosaurus, Postosuchus, Procompsognathus, Riojasaurus, Saltopus, Teratosaurus, Thecodontosaurus*

Distinguishing Features: For the most part, the climate in the Triassic period was hot and dry. The first true mammals appeared during this period, as well as turtles, frogs, salamanders, and lizards. Corals could also be found in oceans at this time, although large reefs such as the ones we have today did not yet exist. Evergreen trees made up much of the plant life.

JURASSIC PERIOD

Date: 208 million to 144 million years ago

Fossils: *Allosaurus, Anchisaurus, Apatosaurus, Barosaurus, Brachiosaurus, Ceratosaurus, Compsognathus, Cryptoclidus, Dilophosaurus, Diplodocus, Eustreptospondylus, Hybodus, Janenschia, Kentrosaurus, Liopleurodon, Megalosaurus, Opthalmosaurus, Rhamphorhynchus, Saurolophus, Segisaurus, Seismosaurus, Stegosaurus, Supersaurus, Syntarsus, Ultrasaurus, Vulcanodon, Xiaosaurus*

Distinguishing Features: The climate of the Jurassic period was warm and moist. The first birds appeared during this period. Plant life was also greener and more widespread. Sharks began swimming in Earth's oceans. Although dinosaurs didn't even exist at the beginning of the Triassic period, they ruled Earth by Jurassic times. There was a minor extinction toward the end of the Jurassic period.

CRETACEOUS PERIOD

Date: 144 million to 65 million years ago

Fossils: *Acrocanthosaurus, Alamosaurus, Albertosaurus, Anatotitan, Ankylosaurus, Argentinosaurus, Bagaceratops, Baryonyx, Carcharodontosaurus, Carnotaurus, Centrosaurus, Chasmosaurus, Corythosaurus, Didelphodon, Edmontonia, Edmontosaurus, Gallimimus, Gigantosaurus, Hadrosaurus, Hypsilophodon, Iguanodon, Kronosaurus, Lambeosaurus, Leaellynasaura, Maiasaura, Megaraptor, Muttaburrasaurus, Nodosaurus, Ornithocheirus, Oviraptor, Pachycephalosaurus, Panoplosaurus, Parasaurolophus, Pentaceratops, Polacanthus, Protoceratops, Psittacosaurus, Quaesitosaurus, Saltasaurus, Sarcosuchus, Saurolophus, Sauropelta, Saurornithoides, Segnosaurus, Spinosaurus, Stegoceras, Stygimoloch, Styracosaurus, Tapejara, Tarbosaurus, Therizinosaurus, Thescelosaurus, Torosaurus, Trachodon, Triceratops, Troodon, Tyrannosaurus rex, Utahraptor, Velociraptor*

Distinguishing Features: The climate of the Cretaceous period was fairly mild. Flowering plants first appeared in this period, and many modern plants developed. With flowering plants came a greater diversity of insect life. Birds further developed into two types: flying and flightless. A wider variety of mammals also existed. At the end of this period came a great mass extinction that wiped out the dinosaurs, along with several other groups of animals.

How to Learn More

At the Library

Cole, Stephen. *Allosaurus! The Life and Death of Big Al.*
New York: Dutton's Children's Books, 2001.

Lambert, David, Darren Naish, and Liz Wyse. *Dinosaur Encyclopedia.*
New York: DK Publishing, 2001.

On the Web

Visit our home page for lots of links about *Allosaurus:*
http://www.childsworld.com/links.html
Note to Parents, Teachers, and Librarians: We routinely verify our
Web links to make sure they're safe, active sites—so encourage
your readers to check them out!

Places to Visit or Contact

AMERICAN MUSEUM OF NATURAL HISTORY
*To view numerous dinosaur fossils, as well
as the fossils of several ancient mammals*
Central Park West at 79th Street
New York, NY 10024-5192
212/769-5100

CARNEGIE MUSEUM OF NATURAL HISTORY
*To view a variety of dinosaur skeletons, as well as fossils related
to other reptiles, amphibians, and fish that are now extinct*
4400 Forbes Avenue
Pittsburgh, PA 15213
412/622-3131

DINOSAUR NATIONAL MONUMENT
To view a huge deposit of dinosaur bones in a natural setting
Dinosaur, CO 81610-9724
or
Dinosaur National Monument (Quarry)
11625 East 1500 South
Jensen, UT 84035
435/781-7700

MUSEUM OF THE ROCKIES
To see real dinosaur fossils, as well as robotic replicas
Montana State University
600 West Kagy Boulevard
Bozeman, MT 59717-2730
406/994-2251 or 406/994-DINO (3466)

NATIONAL MUSEUM OF NATURAL HISTORY
(SMITHSONIAN INSTITUTION)
To see several dinosaur exhibits and special behind-the-scenes tours
10th Street and Constitution Avenue, N.W.
Washington, D.C. 20560-0166
202/357-2700

UNIVERSITY OF WYOMING GEOLOGICAL MUSEUM
To see a cast of Big Al
PO Box 3006
S.H. Knight Geology Building, University of Wyoming
Laramie, WY 82071
307/766-2646

Index

About the Author

Susan H. Gray has bachelor's and master's degrees in zoology, and has taught college-level courses in biology. She first fell in love with fossil hunting while studying paleontology in college. In her 25 years as an author, she has written many articles for scientists and researchers, and many science books for children. Susan enjoys gardening, traveling, and playing the piano. She and her husband, Michael, live in Cabot, Arkansas.